W9-CRD-595

Let It Begin in Me

R. EARL ALLEN

BROADMAN PRESS
Nashville, Tennessee

© Copyright 1985 • Broadman Press
All rights reserved
4250-05
ISBN: 0-8054-5005-X
Dewey Decimal Classification: 242
Subject Headings: MEDITATIONS // CHRISTIAN LIFE
Library of Congress Catalog Card Number: 84-19934
Printed in the United States of America

Library of Congress Cataloging in Publication Data

Allen, R. Earl.
  Let it begin in me.

  Bibliography: p.
  1. Meditations.   I. Title.
BV4832.2.A417   1985   242   84-19934
ISBN 0-8054-5005-X

Contents

Send a revival, O Christ, my Lord,
Let it go over the land and sea,
Send it according to thy dear Word,
And let it begin in me.

Lord, send a revival,
Lord, send a revival,
Lord, send a revival,
And let it begin in me.
                              —B.B. McKinney

1
One Foot in Heaven

That at the name of Jesus every knee should bow,
. . . And that every tongue should confess that
Jesus Christ is Lord, to the glory of God the Father
(Phil. 2:10-11).

Being personally born again is an anticipation of
when all things shall be born again . . . it anticipates
the glorious future and the future glory.
—Bernard L. Ramm[1]

A young actor, already a Christian but bur-
dened with deep conviction of a besetting sin,
walked onto a backcountry bridge and looked
down at the swiftly flowing water. He remem-
bered that the midpoint of the bridge divided
two states. He was divided, too, and couldn't
stand it any longer.

With both arms, he pantomimed lifting a
heavy crate from his inmost being, balancing it
on the rail, and heaving it over. "Now, Lord," he
spoke aloud, "I'm rid of that! Take *all* my life and
use it however You want." He became a gospel
singer.

When we commit ourselves fully to Jesus' lordship, Jesus establishes His rule in our hearts—He
who will rule forever at the right hand of God
the Father. Loving Him here, in a measure as we

7

will love Him there, gives us a foretaste of the essence of eternity. "O what a foretaste of glory divine!"

What does heaven offer? Surely it will ring with joy and praise and abound with beauty. Our glorified Lord will direct our service, each of us joyfully in his or her own place among the select and perfected saints.

If you want to know the happiness of the Lord's divine love here, become absorbed in the Lord Jesus, giving Him pure, wholehearted devotion and response.

> Direct, control, suggest this day
> All I design, or do, or say
> That all my powers, with all their might
> In Thy sole glory may unite.
>   —Thomas Ken

1. Bernard L. Ramm, *Rapping About the Spirit*, p. 52.

2
Don't Say "If"

If thou be the Son of God, come down from the
cross. . . . the centurion, . . . feared greatly, saying,
Truly, this was the Son of God (Matt. 27:40-54).

Jesus Christ, the condescension of divinity and the
exaltation of humanity.　　　　　　　—Phillips Brooks

The history of this world, and every individual
born into it, is preserved in God's books of
record. But according to Revelation 21:27, a
separate book called the Lamb's book of life contains the important names of God's saints. The
basis for inclusion in that book is the answer to
only one question: "What will you do with
Jesus?"

Jesus Christ put similar questions to the disciples: "Whom do men say that I am?" "Whom do
you say that I am?" When Peter declared his
belief in Jesus as Lord—that is, as the almighty
Son of God—Jesus said only God the Father
could have revealed that truth to him.

The debate raged around Jesus' cross. By-
standers at the cross taunted, "If thou be the Son
of God, come down from the cross." Two thieves

chose opposite sides. One chided, "If thou be Christ, save thyself and us." The other pleaded, "Lord, remember me when thou comest into thy kingdom" (Luke 23:39-42). Then the pagan centurion confessed, "Truly this was the Son of God" (v. 54). He made the greatest discovery anyone can make, recognizing the person of the Son of God.

"*If* thou be the Son of God . . ." Down through the ages that *if* has echoed from Calvary, dividing the saved and the lost. Belief in Christ as Son of God and Savior provides the basic building block of the Christian life, the foundation stone of eternal life hereafter.

Holy Spirit, keep me reminded that my assurance of life here and hereafter is bound up with my acknowledgment of Christ as Lord. Amen.

3
Calling Him Lord

Here is the test: no one speaking by the power of
the Spirit of God can curse Jesus, and no one can
say, "Jesus is Lord," and really mean it, unless the
Holy Spirit is helping him (1 Cor. 12:3, TLB).

The ultimate task of the Holy Spirit is to plant the
confession "Jesus is Lord" at the center of every
man's being.   —Jack W. MacGorman[2]

In the process of Christian experience, when
does one receive the Holy Spirit or become filled
with the Spirit? There are different opinions
about this. But the Bible points out one indispu-
table evidence which indicates that the Spirit
controls an individual: calling Jesus Christ Lord
by speech and by life.

Mary, carrying the Child conceived by the
Holy Spirit, exclaimed: "My soul doth magnify
the Lord, and my spirit hath rejoiced in God my
Saviour" (Luke 1:46-47). Jesus was her Savior
and her Lord too.

At salvation, the Holy Spirit applies new life
within, implanting Christ, bringing redemption
of the total self. As we allow Him to work, He
cleanses, controls, and consecrates the driving
urges inside our sinful hearts.

11

A high school principal compared the process of being controlled by the Holy Spirit with four keys he carried to reach the heart of his building —the vault. First, a key for the outside door, one for the main office, another for the principal's office, and then one for the vault. He identified them with four spiritual keys: receiving the Holy Spirit, living in communion with Him, listening to what He says, and obeying Him. Are you using those keys in your life and enthroning Jesus as Lord?

Holy Spirit, so magnify Christ in me that the evidence of His lordship and Your control may abound in my life. Amen.

---

2. Jack W. MacGorman, *The Gifts of the Spirit,* p. 26.

4
Our Best Friend

There is a friend that sticketh closer than a brother
(Prov. 18:24).

In that first Eden, God Himself came down to keep
the man He had made from being lonely. . . .
[Jesus] came to restore fellowship between man
and God, and to take away human loneliness. . . .
He will be your companion and friend.
—Billy Graham[3]

When you were a child, did you cherish a best
friend? Your best friend was the person you
could always count on. If you had a disagree-
ment, your best friend would forgive you and
vice versa. You shared special things with each
other.

As life goes on, sometimes the childhood ability for intimate friendship is lost. But no matter
how old, how rich, how well-educated a person
is, the need for a best friend remains. Today,
there seem to be so many lonely, rootless, friendless people.

The Son of God wants to be our best Friend,
our always-present, always-forgiving, always-
sharing Friend. Jesus loves us forever; Jesus'
friendship is endless; it carries over from this life
into eternity.

Cultivate friendship with Jesus. He fulfills all the deepest meanings of friendship. Spend time with Him, listening to His Word, talking to Him in prayer. Friendship is characterized by the desire to spend time together and share experiences. It would be tragic never to discover the continuing gladness of having Jesus as your ever-present best friend.

Lord Jesus, thank You for being my very best Friend. Help me to seek Your companionship every day and be loyal and faithful, as You are to me. Amen.

---

3. Billy Graham, *Day-by-Day with Billy Graham,* pp. 11-12.

5
The Lord's Friends

Henceforth I call you not servants; for the servant
knoweth not what his lord doeth: but I have called
you friends; for all things that I have heard of my
Father I have made known unto you (John 15:15).

By friendship you mean the greatest love, the
greatest usefulness, the most open communication,
the noblest sufferings, the severest truth, the
heartiest counsel, the greatest union of minds of
which brave men and women are capable.

—Jeremy Taylor

Surely there was a time when all the disciples
proudly claimed they were friends of Jesus of
Nazareth. Yet, in the end, Judas sold Him out,
Peter denied Him, and at Jesus' arrest most of
them fled for their lives like hunted hares.

By any ordinary standard of friendship, they
were failures. Knowing this, Jesus still called
them friends. By Jesus' definition, His complete
sharing with them made them His friends.

If we claim Jesus as our Friend, how do we
treat Him? Jesus' love and loyalty are unques-
tionable. He shared with us not only the words
of God but offered His life. He is utterly truthful
and wise in His dealings with us. Most of all, He
desires to share completely our innermost lives.

How do you measure up as Jesus' friend? Are
you willing to take Jesus with you everywhere?

Do you level with Him and accept His advice? Is your love for Him open and loyal to the point of total risk? Try to live up to His friendship, then you will have a goal worth working toward all your life.

> O Jesus, I have promised
>   To serve Thee to the end;
> Be Thou forever near me,
>   My Master and my Friend.
>   —John E. Bode

6
Trusting God

Trust in him at all times; ye people, pour out your heart before him: God is a refuge for us (Ps. 62:8).

When you have no helpers, see all your helpers in God. When you have many helpers, see God in all your helpers. When you have nothing but God, see all in God; when you have everything, see God in everything.   —Charles H. Spurgeon

A prospector called Limpy found a valuable hoard of silver. It was deep in a cave, and he couldn't dig it out alone. When he found a man strong enough to help, Limpy would tell himself, *That guy's a wrong 'un for sure!* The rest of his life, Limpy lived in poverty, searching in vain for someone he could trust. The problem wasn't that no man could be trusted; it was that the treasure's hiding place was known by a man who was unable to trust.

Any good relationship is based on trust. We need to trust others, to trust ourselves, and especially to trust God. If we don't trust ourselves, we will find it hard to trust others, and that undermines the possibility of good personal and business relationships.

Trust gives access to the resources of others;

and most importantly, it opens our lives to the power of God. Without trust, we stand alone, able to accomplish only what our own meager strength allows. Through trust, we join strength with millions and enter into partnership with God.

Life is a blessed treasure for those who learn to trust in God; it is an empty cave for those who do not. Because God has trusted you with the blessing of life, entrust it back to Him so that He may multiply its blessedness.

Lord Jesus, help me to rely on Your great love, trusting You with all my heart and in all my ways. Amen.

7
The Power of Belief

Jesus said unto him, If thou canst believe, all things
are possible to him that believeth (Mark 9:23).

There are such things as self-fulfilling prophecies. If
one makes a firm resolution, involving mental and
emotional states, and holds onto this at a deep
level, consciously or unconsciously, some kind of
results invariably follow.   —Cecil G. Osborne[4]

Three men were stranded in the desert. One
believed it was possible to walk out; the other
two decided to wait for rescue. The first started
to walk, suffering two days of extreme heat
before he encountered a band of nomads. The
others were never found. One lived because he
put feet to his hope and belief. The other two
waited until death found them.

Life is not always easy, not always good. People aren't always kind. But in the trying times,
belief helps us discover the better possibilities.

The beacon of hope in God shines in the darkness, and its rays of belief point to rescue and
ultimate victory. Because our inner thoughts
and beliefs unconsciously mold our character,
the pattern of one's mind sets the pattern of
behavior. The Lord loves us. As we seek "the

mind of Christ," we see Christ's mighty hand shaping our destinies and guiding our pathways.

Jesus' disciples became pessimists when Jesus died on the cross. But after Pentecost, they became so overwhelmed with the glory of His resurrection that they began to turn "the world upside down" (Acts 17:6).

The risen Christ still provides our immovable foundation for belief. In the Lord Jesus alone is our hope of victory.

Lord Jesus, help me not to surrender to the doubts and pressures of life but to overcome them through faith. Amen.

---

4. Cecil Osborne, *You're in Charge,* p. 90.

8
Shining Stability

Every good gift and every perfect gift is from above, and cometh down from the Father of lights, with whom is no variableness, neither shadow of turning (Jas. 1:17).

Love is ever the beginning of knowledge as fire is of light.
—Thomas Carlyle

Have you ever tried to walk across a familiar room in the dark? Maybe you knew there was nothing in the way, yet your steps faltered and your balance was unsteady. Abundant light is so commonplace you seldom realize how much you depend on it.

A woman who experienced partial loss of sight commented, "People with normal vision can't realize what irritating and dangerous handicaps you encounter when you can't see very well." Without light and clarity, almost every activity is hindered. Light reveals not only form but also color which, along with shape, helps define the world around us in depth and detail.

Without God, we walk in the dark spiritually. The apostle John, introducing Jesus Christ in the first chapter of his Gospel, declared, "That was the true Light, which lighteth every man that cometh into the world" (1:9). If we don't have the light of Christ, we have little spiritual perception of our environment. Our steps hesitate, and our decisions falter.

More important than sunlight is the light of God. Notice that James didn't link God's consistency with judgment but with His mercies. He is the "Father of lights." His rays are as sure as the sun's—if there is nothing between and you have spiritual eyes with which to see. His unchanging love is aware of your needs, and He offers continuing concern. Walk boldly and wisely, therefore, in the light He gives.

Lord Jesus, in Your perfect knowledge, give me clear sight and emotional stability as I lean on Your unchanging love. Amen.

9
The Steadfast Person

He shall be like a tree planted by the rivers of
water, that bringeth forth his fruit in his season; his
leaf also shall not wither; and whatsoever he doeth
shall prosper (Ps. 1:3).

Let us have faith that right makes might, and in that
faith, let us to the end, dare to do our duty as we
understand it.   —Abraham Lincoln

How do you sum up a life? The psalmist wrote
that a righteous man, blessed by God, is like a
tree that grows by a river—like the willows
along the Jordan. Rooted deep in the love of
God, a fruitful Christian life draws nourishment
from the springs of spiritual truth. In the
drought of adversity and hardship, his leaf remains green and his hope doesn't wither.

Cultures other than David's might think of
some different comparisons. In a Texas ranching
community, one man was deeply respected for
his quiet goodness, fair judgment, and understanding toward all. His family held him in high-
est esteem; his children recognized his authority
and obeyed him. From his wife, he received the
truest devotion. His family—and other people
too—depended on his steadfast faith.

23

When he died, many came to his funeral. One of his sons delivered the eulogy. After describing his father's life and character, he summed it up in the sentence, "Dad was like a hitching post; you could tie to him."

In a place and time dependent on horses as transportation, the hitching post was a symbol of immovable security. If it were wood, it would be larger and set deeper than most fence posts. If it were metal or concrete, it would be reinforced so the strongest horse couldn't damage it.

Our Lord Jesus also is like a hitching post. You can "tie to Him."

In our weakness, Lord, may we depend upon your great strength, perfect righteousness, and eternal steadfastness. Amen.

10
Pruning by Pain

The troubles of my heart are enlarged: O bring thou
me out of my distresses. Look upon mine affliction
and my pain; and forgive all my sins (Ps. 25:17-18).

Although today He prunes my twigs with pain,
Yet doth His blood nourish and warm my root:
Tomorrow I shall put forth buds again and clothe
    myself with fruit.   —Christina Rossetti

"If there weren't any pain," many people sigh,
"wouldn't it be wonderful?" Yet pain sometimes
has vital uses.

At times a child is born without the capacity to
feel physical pain. Such a child has to be watched
constantly lest he damage himself and not know
it. Because he feels no pain, he has no warning
of sickness or danger.

Pain can instruct us if we observe carefully. It
can change us for the better, and it can even
save our lives. Once a boy was stubborn about
brushing his teeth. Finally, as he lay awake one
night with a toothache, he talked to himself. *No
more of this! I'm going to take good care of my
teeth so they won't hurt me.* He kept his resolution and continued good dental habits the re-
mainder of his life.

God uses pain and trouble to teach valuable lessons. In God's plan, difficulties become opportunities; but we have to accept them with patience. After we cease to be restless and fretful, we become aware of His kind presence. Trusting Jesus, we can quietly allow Him to remove the hindrances of sin and promote healing and fruit bearing.

Lord Jesus, help me to lift my eyes from the painful things in my life and enjoy Your loving and healing presence. Amen.

11
The Transformed Mind

Be not conformed to this world: but be ye
transformed by the renewing of your mind (Rom.
12:2).

In the depths of our minds there is a fearful
accumulation of every thought, every emotion we
have ever known. The importance lies in what
accumulates. These depths of human personality
need cleansing.   —George Duncan[5]

Defilement comes from within, Jesus taught.
Nothing in our environment can soil us like the
twisted thoughts of our own souls. "A good man
out of the good treasure of the heart bringeth
forth good things, and an evil man out of the evil
treasure bringeth forth evil things" (Matt.
12:35).

The mind is the control center of the body.
Even emotions are controlled by what we tell
ourselves in our minds. If a friend says something cutting, we may fume, *He can't do that to
me!* Or we may tell ourselves, *Poor fellow, he's
having a hard day!* and give him a smile.

Transformation of our minds will change our
natures, characters, and dispositions. If we really
choose to do God's will, the Holy Spirit cleanses,
guides, and remakes us through the Word of

God. He implants the mind of Christ within, upgrading our standards and behavior.

You can choose your own mental shape. Phillips translates Romans 12:2 as follows: "Don't let the world around you squeeze you into its own mould, but let God re-make you so that your whole attitude of mind is changed." It is a continual choice you must make because God's way runs counter to the philosophy of the world. Do you want to be contorted into the pattern of the world, or will you accept the shaping of the Holy Spirit within your redeemed being?

Lord Christ, develop and use my mind for Your glory. Rule my spirit and reveal Your love through me. Amen.

---

5. George Duncan, *Mastery in the Storm,* p. 61.

12
Food for the Mind

Be renewed in the spirit of your mind (Eph. 4:23).

The renewing of our minds occurs in the process of
moving back and forth between the worlds of
hang-loose and hang-tight. All work and no play
makes Jack a dull boy. All play and no work also
makes Jack a vain, self-centered slob.
—James W. Angell[6]

An Old Testament proverb tells us: "As [a man] thinketh in his heart, so is he" (Prov. 23:7).

In our day, research seems to have come full circle and has concluded that much of human illness and trouble is caused by the mind and emotions. In the Bible, the Great Physician has written several prescriptions for our minds.

In Philippians 4:8, God lists six types of food for the mind, nourishment that will keep it strong and healthy. In *The New English Bible* this passage reads: "Now, my friends, all that is true, all that is noble, all that is just and pure, all that is lovable and gracious, whatever is excellent and admirable—fill all your thoughts with these things."

To center the mind on truth, honesty, justice, purity, loveliness, and excellence is positive thinking in its biblical form. You can't control the thoughts which pass through your mind any more than the strangers who knock on your door, but you can refuse to entertain those thoughts and visitors you don't want to encourage. You can reject sordid and critical thinking just as you would spoiled food.

Fresh, delicious, and health-building food is available for your mind as well as your body. Look for it—in the Bible, in conversation, in books, on TV—because the thoughts you entertain build your character and help determine your future.

> May the mind of Christ my Savior,
>   Live in me from day to day,
> By His love and pow'r controlling
>   All I do and say.
> > —Katie B. Wilkinson

---

6. James W. Angell, *Yes Is a Word*, p. 109.

13
Strength from Quietness

In quietness and in confidence shall be your
strength (Isa. 30:15).

Worry and trust cannot live in the same house.
When worry is allowed to come in one door, trust
walks out the other door; and worry stays until trust
is invited in again, whereupon worry walks out.
—R. G. LeTourneau[7]

A catchy modern saying is, "You can't get
there from here." Things look that way to us
when we worry. Wherever we want to go, we
don't see how we can get there from here. Why?
Usually because we refuse to trust God and be
patient. We need to look in the right direction—
to Him.

A traveler in New England hailed a farmer in
a nearby field to ask directions: "How do I get to
Centerville?"

Leaning on his spade handle, the farmer
drawled, "Just two looks from here. You look
where I'm pointin' as fur as you can look. When
you get there you look right, as fur as you can
look. That's Centerville."

Perhaps it takes two looks to get from here to
God: one at yourself as far as you can go. You

have to reach the conclusion you can't make it on your own. Then take a look to the right, toward God, and head for Him.

Look to Christ for the pattern of your life, not to family or friends. God's basic purpose for you is fellowship with Him, and for that you need time to talk and time to listen. Then the Holy Spirit can pour the full potential Christ gives into you and through you.

For strength and guidance to reach your destination, depend on God. Don't fret and worry, for worry is a rip-off. George Washington Lyon commented, "Worry is the interest paid by those who borrow trouble."

Lord Jesus, quiet my fretfulness and teach me to trust You completely. Amen.

---

7. R. G. LeTourneau, *NOW* (Longview, Tex.: LeTourneau Tech).

14
Touchable Things

Seek ye first the kingdom of God, and his
righteousness; and all these things shall be added
unto you (Matt. 6:33).

Life is too great
Between the infant's and the man's estate,
Between the clashing of earth's strife and fate,
For petty things.

—W. M. Vories

The urge to acquire things is human, but nothing else narrows and constricts life like the love of money. If we put money first, we break both the commands Christ summarized from the Commandments: love God and your neighbor.

The person who loves money more than God will certainly find nothing in heaven attractive, for money will be missing. The true treasures of heaven are the fruit of the Spirit, not anything material.

Love of money causes self-chosen slavery of spirit, for such an obsession allows no freedom to love God or others. It leaves no room for appreciation of beauty and goodness. The person who makes money his or her god bows down to an useless golden calf.

What tempts us to love money so much? Usually a distorted need for security. Jesus taught repeatedly, that we are to take no thought for tomorrow. That correctly means, "Don't be anxious!"

Jesus laid out for us a positive goal in life: "Seek ye first the kingdom of God" (Matt. 6:33). If we yearn for, pray for, and work for the kingdom of God, food, clothing, and shelter will be provided as the Heavenly Father sees our need.

If heaven is truly the most important "tomorrow," we are as improvident as grasshoppers if we give ourselves to the immediate things of this world and fail to consider the next.

Lord, continue to remind me that my first priority should be to live at my best spiritually. Amen.

15
How to Enjoy Life

If the Son therefore shall make you free, you shall
be free indeed (John 8:36).

There's something
　　　holy about happiness
　　　healing about smiling
I would like to be
　　　a smiler within the gates
　　　a whistler within the walls.
　　　　　　　　　　　　—Robert A. Raines[8]

Some people approach life with recklessness.
They seek danger boisterously, spurning security. Nothing affronts their determination to be
irresponsible and foolhardy. Their modern pi-
rate ship flies the old flag: "Eat, drink, and be
merry." They think they are getting maximum
gusto out of life, and they call themselves "liberated spirits."

But only Christians are truly free, liberated
spirits. Not only can we act as if we are free but
we can *be* free! The freedom Christ gives produces maximum joy.

Jesus Christ didn't come simply to warn,
"Thou shalt not." God affirmed what we are with
these words, "We [shall] be called the sons of
God" (1 John 3:1). He did not dwell on the fact
that we are weak, sinful, needy, and helpless but

that He has made us heirs of eternity: "Because I live, ye shall live also" (John 14:19). He set us free to live in joy.

When we talk about our faith in God, we should demonstrate this joy. We don't have to look prim and pious. Genuine joy in the Lord witnesses far more effectively than a hundred sermons.

Turn up the corners of your mouth and let life and love shine through your eyes. If you radiate the joy Christ gives, someone is bound to exclaim, "Whatever it is you've got, I want it too!"

Lord Jesus, thank You for the free spirit You have given me. Help me to radiate Your love as I rejoice in Your presence. Amen.

---

8. Robert A. Raines, *Soundings*, p. 115.

16
Who's Perfect?

Be ye therefore perfect, even as your Father which is in heaven is perfect (Matt. 5:48).

"Perfect" in the Bible has three common meanings: full-grown in body or mind, moral completeness or maturity, and moral perfection with particular reference to love as here. To love friends and not enemies is incomplete love, unlike divine love, and leaves us quite imperfect.   —H. Leo Eddleman[9]

In Matthew 5, Jesus listed for the disciples some proper attitudes which, if developed, would lead to genuine Christian holiness. The disciples' righteousness had to exceed that of the scribes and Pharisees, Jesus said, because it should flower from the inner man and not simply be whitewash.

Through God's grace, you and I are intended to be complete and mature, full-grown Christians. All of us need to work on this, but most of all we should surrender to the sculpting of the Holy Spirit who chisels away our weaknesses and imperfections and shapes us into the fullness of God's design.

If you picked a rose and exulted, "See, what a perfect rose!" you wouldn't mean it was a precise copy of an ideal rose. You would mean that

37

it was a good specimen of its own variety and that it had no damaged petals, no limp stem, no sucking aphids.

The exhortations of Jesus, if followed, will enhance your personal uniqueness. He doesn't force you into a mold. Your distinctiveness should be a positive attribute, not a variety of flaws. Through God's grace, you are intended to be with delightful individuality an illustration of Him.

Lord, remold me by Your Spirit and teach me self-discipline so I may exhibit in some measure Your glorious perfection. Amen.

---

9. H. Leo Eddleman, *Teachings of Jesus in Matthew 5-7*, p. 80.

17
Strength for Today

Thy shoes shall be iron and brass; and as thy days, so shall thy strength be (Deut. 33:25).

Each of us may be sure that if God sends us on stony paths, He will provide us with strong shoes. He will not send us out on any journey for which He does not equip us. —*The Megiddo Message*

Full of excitement and enthusiasm, two boys started to climb a high mountain. They were soon exhausted, and their feet were bruised and sore. What had seemed so exciting in prospect proved awfully difficult step by step. Halfway to the top, they gave up.

All life is a day-by-day struggle. Any worthwhile goal is gained only by persistent effort. It's good that God arranged life for us in manageable portions—one day at a time. Usually that's all we can cope with.

Life as a whole offers amazing opportunities and prospects, but often the "daily" seems boring or downright unpleasant. Yet we need to meet each day's challenges head-on with great energy. To finish the job well, we can't afford to slack our effort or waste time. Working or playing, in happiness or sorrow, in wealth or poverty, sickness or health, we must keep our aims high and our spirits undaunted by faith in the Lord Jesus. We need the "strong shoes" that God promised to provide.

We never know what each new day has in store—perhaps unforeseen circumstances and trying setbacks. The best insurance is to begin the day with prayer and reaffirm our faith. Only by faith can we triumph over the unexpected.

The Lord Jesus taught us to ask God for "daily bread," that is, strength for each day.

Heavenly Father, thank You for caring for me each day and giving me the strength I need for each problem of daily life. In Jesus' name, Amen.

18
Saying Thank You

Bless the Lord, O my soul: and all that is within me,
bless his holy name. Bless the Lord, O my soul, and
forget not all his benefits (Ps. 103:1-2).

Life without thankfulness is devoid of love and
passion. Hope without thankfulness is lacking in fine
perception. Faith without thankfulness lacks strength
and fortitude. Every virtue divorced from
thankfulness is maimed and limps along the spiritual
road.   —John Henry Jowett

A young man rescued nineteen people from
the stormy waters of Lake Michigan. He was
recognized for that heroic action and asked,
"What one thing impressed you most during
that experience?"

"The thing that impressed me most about this
whole incident," the young man replied, "was
that not one of the nineteen came back to say
thank you."

When Jesus Christ healed ten lepers—and that
was similar to healing ten terminal cancer pa-
tients today—only one returned to thank Him.

Saying thank you is one of the first courtesies
parents have to teach young children. Often
they forget or get mixed up and say please instead of thank you. Parents or teachers usually

refuse to be satisfied until the child finally responds to a gift with the right words.

God is surely the greatest Giver of gifts. Then should a Christian respond less graciously than a well-trained child? Like a patient parent, God waits to hear your response of gratitude.

You can't claim to live close to the Lord Jesus until you learn to say thank you for all the demonstrations of God's divine love and mercy.

Lord Jesus, thank You. For all You are, for what You have made me, and for what You have given me, thank You. Amen.

19
Miracle Glue

Who shall separate us from the love of Christ? shall
tribulation, or distress, or persecution, or famine, or
nakedness, or peril, or sword? . . . Nay, in all these
things we are more than conquerors through him
that loved us (Rom. 8:35-37).

It is one thing for me to have the Holy Spirit and
quite another for him to have me. Every Christian
has the Holy Spirit, . . . but only as we unwrap our
selfishnesses and yield to him, does his Spirit fully
control our lives.   —Gordon R. McLean[10]

The headline on an ad read "Miracle Glue."
The art work showed a car suspended, presuma-
bly with the glue, from a cable attached to the
roof.

In a sense, God's love is "miracle glue" which
forever holds each of us close to God. We have
received the "Spirit of adoption" by which we
call God Father. The Holy Spirit bears witness to
our relationship with God; God loves us and He
won't "unadopt" us.

Jesus called God Father even on the cross, and
He had every right. "I give unto them eternal
life; and they shall never perish." He promised
concerning His sheep: "My Father, which gave
them me, is greater than all; and no man is able
to pluck them out of my Father's hand" (John
10:28-29).

The marvelous glue in the newspaper ad also carried a warning: "Do not get on skin." If you get it on your finger and touch something, the skin will probably peel off before the glue gives way. Likewise, God's love won't ever release you —the danger is your pulling away from God, thus damaging you.

As you yield to the Holy Spirit, He makes this security an inward reality in your life and continues His work of "perfecting the saints."

Lord Jesus, You know my need for security because You created me that way. Help me always to find my security in You. Amen.

------

10. Gordon R. McLean, *Where the Love Is,* p. 120.

20
DO Fence Me In!

The name of the Lord is a strong tower: the righteous runneth into it, and is safe (Prov. 18:10).

When a person becomes a Christian, he forfeits the right to do what he pleases, . . . this is the meaning of lordship. Christ is to have final authority over all of our lives. He is to be our boss, our manager, our captain, our Lord.   —George E. Worrell[11]

"Don't fence me in!" is an old western saying which became a popular song. People of western heritage, and the independent temperament that often goes with it, often echo that phrase to those who crowd them. Sometimes people find themselves tempted to say that to God.

But God's fences are necessary. God knows what we need and what we don't need. He gives us green pastures and fresh water—provisions for mind and body—as He fences us about with love and blessings. Like a rancher, however, He often has to electrify the fence. Touching an electrified fence, the cattle suffer enough discomfort to warn them against trying to break it down and roam onto the highway or into the bog.

Of course, you may feel as if the devil is the

one fencing you in—maybe he is, if you wandered over into the devil's pasture by disobeying God. But although the devil can wall you around, he can't roof you in. Pray yourself out of the devil's corral and stay inside the Lord's fences. His pastures are broad and bountiful, and you are safe there.

The Lord offers abundant life, full of joy and adventure. If you need to give up some things, He will replace them with superior interests and blessings as you serve Him.

Father, may the standards and motives of my life be truly and firmly grounded in the lordship of Christ. Amen.

---

11. George E. Worrell, ed., *Resources for Renewal,* p. 85.

21
Tested Faith

That the trial of your faith, being much more precious than of gold that perisheth, though it be tried with fire, might be found unto praise and honour and glory at the appearing of Jesus Christ (1 Pet. 1:7).

If God gives faith He will surely try it, and if He leads us out into service and testimony for Him He will surely try us and prove how far we are depending upon Him alone.　　　　—J. R. Caldwell

Elijah declared his faith in God before an audience of thousands on Mount Carmel. He had performed well "on stage"; but after he came down, fear of Jezebel's threats stung his feet, and he ran for days. Finally he collapsed by the brook Cherith and slept. An angel ministered to him until he recovered physically. Then the brook dried up.

"Arise," came the voice of the Lord to Elijah. "Get thee to Zarephath, . . . behold, I have commanded a widow there to sustain thee."

Elijah obeyed. But there was severe drought and famine, and the widow didn't have much to share. By faith, she cooked a meal for the prophet, although she and her son would have to go hungry. Miraculously, "the barrel of meal wasted not, neither did the cruse of oil fail, according to the word of the Lord, which he spake by Elijah" (1 Kings 17:8-16).

Then the widow's faith was also severely tested because her son died. By the power of God, Elijah revived the child and the woman exclaimed, "Now by this I know that thou art a man of God, and that the word of the Lord in thy mouth is truth" (v. 24).

Like them, we may be severely tested, but we must take courage. God will sustain us, perhaps in unexpected responses, and the risen Christ has promised to walk beside us every step of the way.

Lord Jesus, when things look completely impossible to me, remind me that my faith is important not only to me but also to You. Amen.

22
Assistance, Please!

Thou hast been a strength to the poor, a strength to the needy in his distress, a refuge from the storm, a shadow from the heat (Isa. 25:4).

How often we look upon God as our last and feeblest resource! We go to him because we have nowhere else to go. And then we learn that the storms of life have not driven us upon the rocks, but into the desired haven.   —George Macdonald

A boy disobeyed his mother, ate green apples, and became sick. He was reluctant to go home, fearing she would be angry. At last he went to her for help. Seeing her child in pain, the mother showed no anger, only sympathy and concern.

Do we come to God reluctant and ashamed? Even then, He is ready to open the medicine chest full of help and healing.

Do we try everything else before we turn to God? Praying and trusting should come first, not last. Too often, after everything and everybody have failed us, we decide there is nowhere to turn but God. That is not what God intended. Our loving Lord wants us to seek Him first and depend on Him only. When we do, we find He is not only able to meet our needs but able to bless us even beyond that.

Why should we have to prove to ourselves repeatedly that God is the One who can solve our problems? Why should we waste time on less adequate sources? His loving understanding awaits us, along with the fullest measure we can bear of His blessings.

Dear Lord Jesus, thank You for being always available to meet my need and to strengthen me in times of trouble. Help me to call on You first and always. Amen.

23
Private Language

And the Lord came, and stood, and called as at other times, Samuel, Samuel. Then Samuel answered, Speak; for thy servant heareth (1 Sam. 3:10).

When the inner voice is God's voice, not even those dearest to you can convince you otherwise, however pure their intent. The inner peace is past other people's understanding; it is between God and you to meet your special need.   —Jeanette Lockerbie[12]

After a Sunday morning service, two young women dined together. They were extremely quiet until one commented to the other, "Wasn't that a tremendous sermon today?"

"Yes, it really said something to me."

Comparing thoughts, they found that each had been impressed by something different. In both cases, it was an illustration or remark that was not the main theme of the sermon.

Each of us indulges in what the psychologists call "selective attention." R. Lofton Hudson wrote that "we hear that part of the Word of God which speaks particularly to our needs and . . . what we see in the Bible is determined not merely by what is on the pages but by what is in our own anxious heart. We see things not as they are but as we are."[14]

51

Why? Because God made each of us different —in background, parentage, environmental influences—and the longer we live, the more our experiences in life reinforce our uniqueness.

God's messages are filtered through the human personality. To each of us, God encodes His will into "private language"—the impression that affects the individual so that the correct message comes through—the code only you can understand. Of course, God never denies Himself or His Word, the Bible. But if you listen prayerfully—"Speak Lord; for Thy servant heareth"—He will give you the message to meet your need.

Father, thank You for speaking to me in the ways I can best understand. Guide me so I may reflect the Lord Jesus. Amen.

---

12. Jeanette Lockerbie, *Fifty Plus,* p. 65.

24
Standing Alone

At my first answer no man stood with me, but all men forsook me: I pray God that it may not be laid to their charge. Notwithstanding the Lord stood with me, and strengthened me; . . . and I was delivered (2 Tim. 4:16-17).

It is human to stand with the crowd. It is divine to stand alone. It is manlike to follow the people, to drift with the tide; it is Godlike to follow a principle, to stem the tide.   —Author Unknown

Because the apostle Paul had believed and taught contrary to Roman policy, he was taken before Nero. Paul's life stood in jeopardy. Paul stood alone. But he was in no case the only person in the Bible who stood alone.

Noah's neighbors laughed while he labored to build a strange ship called an ark. Abraham left Ur and worshiped God among heathen neighbors. Daniel prayed alone in Babylon while his enemies listened and plotted against him. Elijah sacrificed to God alone on the mountain while Queen Jezebel and four hundred prophets of Baal taunted him. Jeremiah prophesied that God would punish His people and wept alone over Jerusalem.

Jesus loved and died alone, and He cautioned the disciples, "If ye were of the world, the world

53

would love his own, but because ye are not of the world, . . . therefore the world hateth you" (John 15:19).

Multitudes today, both in the church and in the world, applaud the courage of these ancient prophets and martyrs but condemn similar faithfulness today as stubbornness or foolishness. Do you dare stand alone for God? Will you really be all by yourself if you do? No, for as He did with Paul, the Lord will stand with you.

Lord Jesus, may I obey my convictions of truth and duty, even at the cost of fortune, friends, and life itself. Amen.

25
Enemies Nearby!

A man's foes shall be they of his own household
(Matt. 10:36).

Wounds inflicted by those who may dislike—or even
hate us—hurt, are understandable. Wounds by those
we love hurt to the core—and are incomprehensible.
Charles Haddon Spurgeon expressed it: "The sins
of the unbeliever plunge the spear into Christ's side;
the sins of the Christian thrust the spear into His
heart." How often we harm the very people we love
the most!   —Author Unknown

A woman's husband encouraged her to make
a profession of faith in Christ. When she did, she
made up her mind to be all that God wanted her
to be. Her husband couldn't accept that kind of
commitment because he no longer felt he was
the "boss" in her life. One day when she started
to church, he pushed her down a flight of stairs,
injuring her severely.

If you really stand tall for Christ, somebody at
home may not like it. Experience has taught
many a Christian that "a man's foes shall be they
of his own household." If your life is different
because you are living out your commitment to
Christ, that serves as a rebuke to those who are
not deeply committed.

Christians who put Christ first find more ridi-
cule and persecution from other Christians who

are not deeply committed than they do from unsaved people! Our "friendly foes" can do us more harm than anyone else. Those near and dear to us can upset us most. Our loved ones have free access to our hearts while we are fortified against our recognized enemies.

When you make Christ genuine Lord of your life, your basic human loneliness may be intensified, for you march to a beat that those around you can't hear. If you are called odd because of your loyalty to the Lord Jesus, you may be sure you will at last hear God say, "Well done!"

Holy Spirit, help me to be true to Christ, even when no one else understands, and to stand tall for Him, no matter the cost. Amen.

26
Ladder of Confidence

We can rejoice, too, when we run into problems and trials for we know that they are good for us—they help us learn to be patient. And patience develops strength of character in us and helps us trust God more each time we use it until finally our hope and faith are strong and steady (Rom. 5:3-4, TLB).

Dedication is not simply yielding all—it is taking all. Someone has said that it is not what we give to Jesus but what we take from Him that makes us strong and victorious day by day.   —Alan Redpath[13]

A faithful Christian woman came home from the hospital thin and wan faced after difficult major surgery. "There was a lot of pain," she admitted to a visitor, "but God sprinkled through it many beautiful moments to make it more bearable—and now I'm getting well."

In all our trials, we should likewise look for God's hand in the situation and realize our opportunity to experience His love more deeply.

The apostle Paul outlined certain steps which will lead us from despair to victory. We begin at the bottom with suffering, pressure, and trouble. Through these we learn to reach the first rung of the ladder: patience. The next step produces strength of character—that is, a mature attitude of endurance. As we continue, we learn that confident hope in God will never disappoint us.

Joyful faith is at the top of the ladder. This is a gift of God, but we must reach up to take it from Him.

The ladder of confidence doesn't end in a small platform on which we must balance but on a new level of living. The spiritual foundations upon which we build our hope and faith hold strong and steady. Experience of the love of God, flowing through us by the Holy Spirit, gives a feeling of security nothing can shake.

Lord Jesus, keep me looking up to You as I endure the struggles of life and keep climbing. Amen.

---

13. Alan Redpath, *Victorious Christian Service,* p. 174.

27
The End Product

I am sure that God who began the good work within you will keep right on helping you grow in his grace until his task within you is finally finished on that day when Jesus Christ returns (Phil. 1:6, TLB).

Go over your life and see where there are loose ends, broken promises, half-fulfilled tasks; and begin to complete the uncompleted, fulfill the half-fulfilled, and gather up the loose ends; and when you do so, there will be a sense of well-being, a sense of being whole.
—E. Stanley Jones[14]

Are you a half-finished person? Every Christian lives uncompleted, as the popular slogan goes: "Be patient, God isn't finished with me yet."

The Holy Spirit was instrumental in our salvation, and He will bring to completion the spiritual life He implanted. Our part is continuing surrender. As we say yes to the indwelling Spirit, He keeps on working within us until He presents us cleansed and "faultless before the presence of [God's] glory with exceeding joy" (Jude 24).

Here is a paradox: God must work, and we must work also. In day-to-day living, we may have a "finishing" problem that hinders our growth. Most of us try to take on too much and often do a shoddy, hurried job or don't complete it at all. The debris of life mounts up and swallows us; the shirked chores, unfinished projects, and broken promises paralyze us. A haunting sense of incompleteness can account for tension which makes us unable to relax and be at peace in the Lord.

Does your life ride off in all directions? Or is it simplified and given shape by the Spirit's guidance? As you find your focus in Christ, the Holy Spirit can work freely to "put it all together" and make you more like Him.

Lord Jesus, forgive me for cluttering up my life and help me become what You intended me to be. Amen.

---

14. E. Stanley Jones, *The Art of Mastering Life,* p. 189.

28
Look in the Mirror

But we all, with open face beholding as in a glass the glory of the Lord, are changed into the same image from glory to glory, even as by the Spirit of the Lord (2 Cor. 3:18).

We whom the Spirit blessed with His gifts are the mirror of the Lord, the bright surface on which the grace of His lordship is reflected.

—Martin H. Franzmann[15]

When you have a photograph made, you may think that proofs come in only two varieties: poor and terrible. Do you suppose God sometimes feels like that about us? We are meant to be God's representatives; we should reflect the Lord's likeness in our lives so others may see Him.

Non-Christians around us probably won't read the Bible, but they do watch us. Often our reflection of our Lord is the only bit of God they see. If we distort that reflection like a damaged mirror, how can they know Him?

Harold E. Dye tells how his wife was using a public copying machine when an old Mexican woman looked over her shoulder: "What ees that you do?"

"I'm making copies of some pages from this

book. Here, I'll show you." She repeated the process with another page. "The old woman gazed at the paper for a moment and whispered, '*Esta bueno*—ees good, ees wonderful machine; ees like *Dios*—like God?' "

"Like God?" asked Mrs. Dye.

" '*Si*—like God. Een God's book, *la Biblia*, eet ees say that God can make us to look like Christ. That ees what the Bible say that God can do.' "[16]

He can if we let Him. Often we are unsure exactly who we are and have even less an idea what we should be. But the Holy Spirit holds up Christ to us as our model. Day by day we should look at Him and thereby come to resemble Him more and more.

Holy Spirit, do Your great work in me! Make me over into the likeness of Jesus Christ my Lord. Amen.

15. Martin H. Franzmann, *Alive with the Spirit*, p. 47.

16. Harold H. Dye in *Open Windows* (Nashville: The Sunday School Board of the Southern Baptist Convention, 1976).

29
Seeds of Conflict

For God hath not given us the spirit of fear; but of
power, and of love, and of a sound mind
(2 Tim. 1:7).

Fear contains the seeds of every conflict, whether it
be personal, social, or international.
. . . fear is an emotion and only other emotions
can deal with it: trust, love, faith.   —Paul Tournier[17]

Early in the Bible God started educating the
people about fear. God's purpose was to protect
them against that often-used weapon of the
devil. God commanded again and again in the
Old Testament, "Fear not!" He had to repeat it
over and over to each of His chosen leaders.

When the Israelites fled before the Egyptian
army and came to the Red Sea, God ordered,
"Fear not, stand still, and see the salvation of the
Lord." After they obeyed, God instructed Moses,
"Speak unto the children of Israel, that they go
forward" (Ex. 14:13-15).

After Moses' death, God also encouraged
Joshua to go forward: "Have I not commanded
thee? Be strong and of a good courage; be not
afraid, neither be thou dismayed: for the Lord

thy God is with thee whithersoever thou goest"
(Josh. 1:9).

Centuries later, God spoke similar words to
Isaiah when that young nobleman was disturbed
because his king had died. "Fear thou not, for I
am with thee: be not dismayed; for I am thy God.
I will strengthen thee; yea, I will help thee; yea,
I will uphold thee with the right hand of my
righteousness" (Isa. 41:10).

In the New Testament when Christ appeared
to the apprehensive disciples whose boat
seemed swamped, He said, "It is I; be not afraid"
(John 6:20). Then on the eve of Christ's crucifix-
ion, still trying to quiet their fears, He began to
discuss the future with, "Let not your heart be
troubled, neither let it be afraid" (John 14:27).

Lord Jesus, help me to trust You and not let
the seeds of conflict and fear sprout in my
life. Amen.

---

17. Paul Tournier, *Escape from Loneliness,* p. 187.

30
Worth Repeating

Rejoice in the Lord alway, and again I say, Rejoice.
(Phil. 4:4).

[Joy] is not something you can work up, but
something that the Lord imparts to His children. It is
a fruit of the Spirit, . . . Let Him fill you, and joy will
be as natural as the murmur of a stream as it flows.
—Alan Redpath[18]

On which side of the ledger should a Christian
list personal tribulations and trials? We hear
James, the half-brother of Jesus, answer from the
midst of persecution, Count it on the joy side—
"count it all joy" (Jas. 1:2).

Within the shadow of the cross, Jesus gathered
the disciples and talked to them about joy.
"These things have I spoken unto you, that my
joy might remain in you, and that your joy might
be full" (John 15:11). The joy He wanted for
them went deeper than bubbling good humor; it
was the abiding certainty of triumph.

How were the disciples supposed to achieve
joy? Like the joy of Jesus Himself, which came
from Jesus' complete trust in the Father, joy
would be the gift of God when certain conditions
were met.

The road to joy goes first through the gates of trust. No amount of trouble can shake those who depend on God. I've heard that we should never face trouble without first thanking God for it. Then, somehow that trouble becomes an opportunity. Our hearts will experience the refreshing of God: quiet pools of peace, rippling brooks of thankfulness, and fountains of rejoicing.

Paul's exhortation to "Rejoice in the Lord" bears repeating every day.

Lord, share with me Your gift of joy. Let my life exhibit it in Christlikeness, along with the other fruit of the Spirit. Amen.

18. Redpath, p. 146.

31
This Time, This Place

The vessel that he made of clay was marred in the
hand of the potter, so he made it again another
vessel, as seemed good to the potter to make it
(Jer. 18:4)

Life is an infinite series of new beginnings because
God's love is an infinite series of forgivenesses and
accomodations of his plan for our limitations and
failures. Lovingly, patiently, he presents to us each
moment a new plan that is possible of fulfillment,
beginning at the place where we now stand.
—Lionel A. Whiston[19]

Each day is a new beginning. Every morning
we should ask, "What is God's will for me today?" That is one meaning of revival—a new
obedience.

For each of us, three Bible basics outline God's
will. First, the decision to live for Christ: God
wants us to know the Son. Second, in this time of
twisted values, what Paul wrote still stands:
"God wants you to be holy and pure" (1 Thess.
4:3, TLB). He wants our desires aligned with
holiness.

Then God wants us to have direction in our
lives. We need to outgrow yesterday and keep
moving. He can steer us only when we're moving. Cars without power steering have difficulty
turning unless they are in gear and under way.

God doesn't accept the answer, "Someday."

He urges, "Now is the accepted time." He determines the right time and place for each obedience; if we are going to do God's will, it must be at His appointed time.

We begin by believing that God will guide us and by accepting God's direction. From those who demand to know His will before they decide whether they'll obey, He conceals His plans. It's best to say yes and let Him lead.

Lord, I will to do Your will. In my blind strivings, reveal Yourself and lead me each new day. Amen.

19. Lionel A. Whiston, *Enjoy the Journey*, p. 35.

32
Ready for Anything

I know both how to be abased, and I know how to
abound: . . . I can do all things through Christ which
strengtheneth me (Phil. 4:12-13).

There is something in a person's inability to accept
what has happened in the natural course of things
which is akin to turning down God's sovereignty in
his life.   —Jeanette Lockerbie[20]

A group of men were planning a mountain
expedition. The day before they left, they had a
"shakedown"—a time when they checked to see
if they had all the equipment they needed and
if it were ready for the tasks ahead. They wanted
to make sure they were able to meet the strenu-
ous conditions they would encounter on the
mountain.

Such precautions are wise. The familiar Boy
Scout motto "Be prepared" teaches this truth.

During World War II, the British were ex-
ceedingly proud of their Royal Air Force (RAF)
which defended them from the Nazis. They
talked constantly about their RAF. Later an
English pastor rearranged the letters to form a
slogan with which to challenge his church mem-
bers: R.F.A.—"Ready For Anything," like the

apostle Paul. Ready in faith, ready in patience, ready in prayer, ready in witness, ready in sharing—these were listed as some of the ways we should be prepared as Christians.

Unforeseen circumstances threaten the course of every life, and tomorrow always holds mysteries. Only God knows what lies ahead, and He will train and equip us. God's provisions may seem strange at times, but in His wisdom He provides for our future needs.

God gave us a road map, the Bible, together with daily sources of strength. The apostle Paul affirmed, "I have learned, in whatsoever state I am, therewith to be content" (Phil. 4:11). He could make both privation and prosperity stepping stones in spiritual growth and in the service of God. Can we?

Lord, give me the courage to follow Paul's example and testify, "I have learned how to get along happily whether I have much or little" (TLB). Amen.

---

20. Lockerbie, p. 15.

33
Don't Worry, Don't Forget!

Don't worry about anything; instead, pray about
everything; tell God your needs and don't forget to
thank him for his answers (Phil. 4:6, TLB).

The response of thanksgiving and praise to God
seemingly releases a power beyond our ability to
comprehend. . . . I tried "thanks therapy" and found
that it works.   —Jeanette Lockerbie[21]

When Paul wrote "Don't worry about anything," surely he couldn't have been talking to
us with all our problems! But he was—he includ-
ed every child of God! In the next verse Paul's
purpose is explained: "His peace will keep your
thoughts and your hearts quiet and at rest as you
trust in Christ Jesus" (4:7, TLB).

We can put that promise to work by following
the exhortation at the end of verse 6: "Don't
forget to thank him for his answers!" That is, we
are to thank Him beforehand for the answers we
trust will come.

Sometimes we tell ourselves we can't cope,
and we have little hope that God can either. We
may rebel against circumstances and resent trials, unable to see their value in aiding our Christian growth. Or we may look on the negative

side and refuse to feel, enjoy, or attempt to accomplish anything for fear of failure.

When life looks dark, we aren't inclined to praise God or anybody else. Only the prompting of the Holy Spirit within can enable us to do it. We should tell God our needs, believing He can and will supply them. Then we thank Him for what He's accomplishing in our lives, both in answer to prayer and for our Christian growth.

Lord Jesus, in the dimness of my confusion, thank You for the promise of light. Keep me grateful and believing. Amen.

---

21. Ibid., p. 32.

34
God's Priorities

Let no one interfere with me after this, for I bear
branded on my body the owner's stamp of the Lord
Jesus (Gal. 6:17, Moffatt).

I am the Lord's! Yet teach me all it meaneth,
All it involves of love and loyalty,
Of holy service, absolute surrender,
And unreserved obedience unto Thee.
—Lucy A. Bennett[22]

The lordship of Christ requires that He have first place in the life of every Christian. This priority sometimes causes sticky problems, especially for those who are dedicated to a specific Christian service. Always there are some—family, friends, and sometimes the friendless—who make demands that take time and energy away from God's assigned tasks.

In the face of such demands, what is the Christlike attitude? Is the only Christian response total giving in to the demands of others? Many seem to think so; others will often tell you so!

Yet Christ demands top priority. Sometimes we must refuse even our loved ones, like Jesus did in Cana when He was first asked and more emphatically in Capernaum: "My mother and my brethren are these who hear the word of God, and do it" (Luke 8:21).

A young, single missionary on furlough shared the problem she had encountered with her Christian parents when she made plans to enter the mission field. "My mother fought it every step of the way," she noted. "It wasn't at all what she wanted for me, and my father went along with her." But after the daughter had gone, a friend overheard her father reporting with obvious pride, "My daughter is a missionary."

Lord Jesus, when others would make seemingly unwarranted claims upon my life and time, help me to discern Your will and to resist all claims that are not Your claims. Amen.

---

22. Lucy A. Bennett, *Hymns,* Paul Beckwith, ed., #143.

35
What's Valuable?

Let every man learn to assess properly the value of
his own work and he can then be rightly proud when
he has done something worth doing, without
depending on the approval of others
(Gal. 6:4, Phillips).

Determine beforehand to lay at the feet of Jesus
both praise and blame.   —E. Stanley Jones[23]

In church life, agreeability and submission are
highly regarded and considered signs of Christian humility. But these traits can also indicate
apathy or indifference. To be a contributor instead of a pew sitter, one must have a firm sense
of one's own individuality and value system.

Neither criticism nor praise should control us,
although both can be useful for learning. When
we were children, we were dependent upon our
parents, and their approval was crucial to our
development. But we can't mature as persons
without learning to think for ourselves.

The controlling factor in our behavior should
be our own personal set of values, derived from
God's Word and subject to His guidance. Our
actions grow out of our values. If what others
think becomes overly important, we may try too

hard to please and be more likely to fail than to succeed. It is possible to lose our integrity and the respect of others as well.

Look again at how Paul described the proper Christian attitude: *"assess properly* the value of his own work" (author's italics). It helps to remember that we are God's beloved children and therefore important to Him. Then we must try to understand where we fit into His plan, what we can contribute, and whether we are using our full potential.

O Lord, teach me to adopt and act on Your values so my life will glorify You. Amen.

23. Jones, *Growing Spiritually,* p. 83.

36
Shut the Door

Whatsoever God doeth, it shall be for ever: . . . God requireth that which is past (Eccl. 3:14-15).

In repentance, a person gets a new mind about his conduct. He not only sees that he committed a wrong act, but he admits that the reason he did it was because he had the wrong attitude toward God.
—R. Lofton Hudson[24]

Many Christians feel that serious mistakes in the past disqualify them for any part in God's service. A woman in her thirties was trying to build a new life for herself after being divorced. She found an open door into Christian work, but she hesitated. An older woman pointed out a Scripture verse the divorcee had never before seen: "God requireth that which is past."

Thoughtfully the young woman read and re-read it, then noticed in the previous verse, "Whatsoever God doeth, it shall be forever." To her that seemed contradictory. "How can we leave the past behind if God remembers it forever?" she argued.

"When we repent, God forgives the sins in our past," her friend pointed out. "We must leave it all with Him, and He will lift the burden. If God

77

is in your calling and you walk into the future with faith in Him, your past will not hinder you."

God requires that we relinquish the past to Him and go forward. Even good things and happy times, if we cling to them and try to relive them, can hinder our growth. When we face our problems and our past and turn them all over to God, we find ourselves on the road to a happier, healthier, and more effective future with God as our controlling partner.

Lord Jesus, thank You for accepting me and cleansing my past. Discard the useless and equip me for future service. Amen.

---

24. R. Lofton Hudson, *Helping Each Other Be Human,* p. 135.

37
Making Life Livable

Beside this, giving all diligence, add to your faith virtue; and to virtue knowledge; And to knowledge temperance; and to temperance patience; and to patience godliness (2 Pet. 1:5-6).

The question my people asked was, "What is the recipe for continual renewal?" The answer is a disciplined life. Discipline is a tough business—much tougher than abstinence, which we would prefer for simplicity's sake. —Tom Brandon[25]

Have you watched a public building, perhaps your church, being constructed? First, the foundations go down, then the framework rises. Brick or stone follows, and when the roof goes on, it's "in the dry" at last. But it's not "in the warm." There remains the arduous task of closing in the building.

To construct our Christian lives, we must lay the foundation of faith. Living a good life and knowing God better help us erect the superstructure—the framing, walls, floors, roof.

In this time of energy shortages, insulation is an important item. Temperance is the insulation in our house of life—the disciplined balance of putting aside our own desires and not letting people and circumstances make us hot or cold. It has been established that protection from cold and heat definitely promotes more efficient work.

Our building will soon deteriorate without the upkeep of patience. Patience is a necessary ingredient for the crowning glory of the finished building—godliness, which is allowing God to fill our lives. Then we can hold "open house," where others are invited in and ministered to by God through us.

It requires continual effort to build our Christian lives, and we must refer constantly to God's plans. The required discipline isn't easy, but our willingness to submit to it determines our success.

Lord Jesus, help me be disciplined so my house of life may be a worthy temple for You. Amen.

---

25. Tom Brandon in Worrell, p. 46.

38
Forget to Remember

This one thing I do, forgetting those things which are behind, and reaching forth unto those things which are before, I press toward the mark for the prize of the high calling of God in Christ Jesus (Phil. 3:13-14).

Rather than live in regret over the past, give God your "second best" and let Him make a success of your new beginning.　　　—P. Kenneth Geiser, MD[26]

A young doctor met a missionary doctor on furlough and confided that he himself had planned to become a missionary. At the last moment, he changed his plans because of his parents' objections. "I've lived in regret ever since," he mused.

What comfort could you offer such a person? Maybe you have had a similar experience. Often it is too late to backtrack and pick up the thread of what you believe was God's best for your life.

The apostle Paul suggested how to overcome this problem.

First, don't drown in a pool of regrets. Saul of Tarsus rejected God's calling until the risen Christ stopped him forcibly on the road to Damascus. Paul certainly had much over which to grieve, having persecuted many Christians.

Second, take stock of the present and the future. Notice Paul's verbs: "reaching forth" and "press toward." Neither positions nor jobs matter as much as our "high calling"—the privilege of participating with Christ in Christ's work.

Our loving Lord will put to the best possible use whatever talents and abilities we surrender to Him now, no matter how completely we have failed in the past. God does not want us to grieve over what might have been or over what we have to offer now, even though it seems to us "second best." We must be willing to walk through the doors He opens for us at present.

Holy Spirit, keep ever before me the goal of being like the Lord Jesus so I may forget the past and press on. Amen.

---

26. P. Kenneth Geiser, M.D., in Osborne, p. 90.

39
Shortcuts

Then saith Jesus unto him, Get thee hence, Satan:
for it is written, Thou shalt worship the Lord thy
God, and him only shalt thou serve (Matt. 4:10).

They tell the story of a boy who "helped" a butterfly
to emerge by cutting a hole in the chrysalis, only to
discover that he had been in too much of a hurry.
The butterfly was not ready, and could not fly.
Emerging Christians, too, can't be rushed, but must
face their own inner struggles and grow until their
wings are strong enough to fly.   —Walden Howard[27]

Jesus met and conquered, in the third temptation, the most subtle snare of the devil. Satan offered a shortcut to Jesus' goal, the reclaiming of His creation. When the devil can find no other vulnerable spot in a Christian, he makes his most tempting offer: "I will give you the worthwhile object of your desire, and mine is the easy way."

The world has a slogan for it: The end justifies the means. If you want good grades, the devil suggests cheating. If you want business success, the devil suggests dishonesty and using others. If you want happiness, the devil suggests seeking it selfishly in worldly and immoral pleasure. Many people learn too late that these methods don't achieve their goals because the devil himself is a liar and a cheat.

God's way is: "Seek ye first the kingdom of

God and His righteousness." To receive good grades, pray and study hard. To achieve success in business or profession, pray much, work hard, and be honest. Inner peace and real achievement are not accidents—they are fruit grown by patient cultivation and ripened by the loving kindness of God.

We must dare to put our hand in God's and walk straight ahead.

Lord, give me wisdom to approach my goals through seeking You first that I may come into Your presence with joy. Amen.

---

27. Walden Howard, *Nine Roads to Renewal,* p. 32.

40
Talented People

And he saith unto them, Follow me, and I will make you fishers of men (Matt. 4:19).

God never gives a man a job without first making that man into the person suited for the job and properly equipped. —Gordon R. McLean[28]

God doesn't give training or talent to be wasted. All that you have can be used for His glory, no matter how improbable your combinations of interests may seem. As Dr. Clyde Narramore observed, "Your natural abilities are God's suggestions for your life's work."

Yet there are those who apparently have deemphasized the use of a natural abilities to serve God another way. Albert Schweitzer, a virtuoso on the organ, renounced the concert halls for surgery in the Congo jungles. His marvelous musical talent seemed wasted in Africa, but it enabled him to finance his own hospital, and his fame as an organist carried knowledge of his sacrificial mission work all over the world.

Do we hesitate to commit ourselves to God's will, fearing it will clash with our own ambitions?

Yet God knows us far better than we know ourselves. If we serve God and minister to others according to the gift we have received from Him, then He takes care of the results. If we allow Him to guide, He will lead into the widest possible usefulness and blessing.

Everyone has one talent—to be what God intended. Right where you are, God can enable you to do your particular job of living better than anyone else. You are responsible to discover new dimensions of God's creative love for someone in your particular situation.

Lord Jesus, You made me. Please equip me for the job You have for me that I may glorify You more completely. Amen.

---

28. McLean, p. 173.

41
Planned Neglect

One thing is needful: and Mary hath chosen that
good part, which shall not be taken away from her
(Luke 10:42).

As you walk along with the Holy Spirit, balanced
upon the two legs of prayer and the Word, He will
lead you down a path named, "the will of God."
—Ray E. Baughman[29]

A young concert violinist was asked the secret of her success. "Planned neglect," she replied.

Then she explained, "When I was in school, there were many things that demanded my time. When I went to my room after breakfast, I made my bed, straightened the room, dusted the floor, and did whatever else came to my attention. Then I turned to my violin practice.

"I found I wasn't progressing as I thought I should, so I reversed things. Until my practice period was completed, I deliberately neglected everything else. That program of planned neglect, I believe, accounts for my success."

Jesus challenged, "Seek ye first the kingdom of God" (Matt. 6:33). Paul asserted, "This one thing I do" (Phil. 3:13). We have to choose what is of greatest importance and learn to say no or "later" to other matters. If we try to do everything, we may find ourselves unable to do anything well. The road to accomplishment in any area lies between the walls of commitment and priority. For a Christian, this means putting the Lord Jesus first.

If we fail to find God's will and to act in harmony with it, we may react to life with feelings of pressure and bitterness. If we allow negative forces to dictate our decisions, we are at the mercy of circumstances.

First of all, we must listen to the Lord Jesus, which is "that good part, which shall not be taken away." Then we can meet challenges and circumstances as if they were God's appointments—that's how we stay in God's will and do our best for Him.

Holy Spirit, keep me listening, praying, and walking in the will of God. Amen.

---

29. Ray E. Bauman, *The Abundant Life,* p. 61.

42
Success Begins Here

This book of the law shall not depart out of thy mouth; but thou shalt meditate therein day and night, that thou mayest observe to do according to all that is written therein, for then thou shalt make thy way prosperous, and then thou shalt have good success (Josh. 1:8).

Success or failure . . . is caused more by mental attitudes than by mental capabilities.
—Walter Dill Scott, M.D.[30]

One of God's earliest prescriptions for godly and successful living was given to Joshua. Appointed to follow Moses in leading the Israelites into the Promised Land, Joshua was instructed by God to know, meditate on, and obey God's commandments.

In the Christian life, God's Word has three functions. It cleanses our minds, corrects our wrong attitudes, and guides our paths—besides providing information. Most Christians know too little about personal contact with God, especially about seeking and securing God's guidance. We are prone to tumble from event to event in life without spiritual perception, and we often have no sense of working out a life plan under God's direction.

"It is the vocation that creates the person,"

commented Professor Richard Siebeck. Dr. Paul Tournier, famous Swiss Christian doctor and writer, added, "The converse is also true, however: often, in order to discover what one's vocation is, it is necessary first to become a person through the intimate dialogue with God, which is what meditation is."[31]

As Christians, our primary commitment is to God's will; we can never succeed without a sense of mission. God plants and nourishes our calling in our heart. If we willingly serve Him in the place to which He calls us, we find not only blessing and contentment but also an increased capacity to serve.

Lord, help me listen to You carefully, obey You implicitly, leaving the outcome to You. Amen.

30. Walter Dill Scott, M.D., in Osborne, p. 89.
31. Tournier, *The Adventure of Living,* p. 220.

43
Building Stones

O thou afflicted, tossed with tempest, and not comforted, behold, I will lay thy stones with fair colours, and lay thy foundations with sapphires (Isa. 54:11).

Never mind all the contributing factors and the other people involved in what has hurt you. Just believe that God wants to bless you. He will take care of how He's going to do it.   —Jeanette Lockerbie[32]

Submission to suffering and the expectation of deliverance from it are equally the fruit of faith.

In Bible times, great buildings were constructed with quarried stone. Some of the stones from the Temple built about 400 BC still stand in Jerusalem—the famous "wailing wall" of the Jews.

The apostle Peter talked about the church being built of "living stones"—that is, Christian individuals fitted together (1 Pet. 2:4-6). If we also are stones, what can we learn from those building blocks of God's Temple in Jerusalem?

"We come from distant mountains, from the sides of craggy hills," they might say to us. "Wind and water buffeted us for ages and left us only ragged cliffs. Human hands reshaped some of us into a dwelling place for God. Others became buildings where the children of your race were born and found rest and shelter and suffered and rejoiced and learned the lessons set for them by our Creator and yours.

"We suffered much travail being fitted for our places," they would tell us. "We were hacked roughly from our beds; pickaxes cleaned and seamed us. Gradually we were chiseled into blocks, and some of us were polished until one side gleamed in the sunlight. Now we are complete and in our places and of service.

"You are in the quarry still, and not complete," they could say to us. "To you as once to us, much is mysterious. But you are destined for a higher building, and one day you will be placed in it by hands not human, a living stone in a heavenly temple."

> Great Sculptor, hew and polish us; nor let,
> Hidden and lost, Thy form within us lie.
> —Author Unknown

---

32. Lockerbie, p. 34.

44
"Strengthen My Hands"

They all made us afraid, saying, Their hands shall
be weakened from the work, that it be not done.
Now therefore, O God, strengthen my hands
(Neh. 6:9).

Nehemiah triumphed because he was doing a work
which God initiated, and because God initiated it,
God Himself empowered it. It would never have
succeeded unless God had begun it; unless the
origin of this work had been in the heart of God, it
would never have been in the heart of Nehemiah.[1]
—Alan Redpath[33]

The Old Testament Book of Nehemiah provides us a profitable object lesson in Christian service. When Nehemiah received a firsthand report that Jerusalem was in a terrible state of disrepair, Nehemiah's heart was touched. First, he prayed to God; then he approached the king in whose palace he served and who must have respected him. He asked for and received permission to repair the walls of Jerusalem and also a safe-conduct pass and provisions for his journey.

Nehemiah's first project was to rebuild the walls which had fallen down. In this he persevered through numerous setbacks and attacks by many enemies. Each time Nehemiah assumed a firm, positive stand and prayed, "O God, strengthen my hands"!

How often, believing we were called of God to a special task, we find ourselves exhausted or with obstacles we can't seem to overcome. It is easy to conclude that we were not called to do that task, after all, and somebody else had better take it over. Nehemiah completed his task in spite of discouraged employees and clever enemies because he was willing to persevere. He didn't ask God for a way out—only for strength to finish the work.

Do you sometimes question God's willingness to back you up? Seek out the work God has for you, and He will not only bless and strengthen you, but He will go ahead to prepare the way.

Lord Jesus, may my life show the same mixture of prayer and wise action as Nehemiah's. Amen.

---

33. Redpath, p. 124.

45
The Wise Farmer

In the morning sow thy seed, and in the evening
withhold not thine hand; for thou knowest not
whether shall prosper, either this or that, or whether
they both shall be alike good (Eccl. 11:6).

A crisis brings out all of our spiritual and mental
resources into sharp focus, but faith is never born in
a crisis. One who awaits disaster before learning the
meaning of prayer is in for a shock.
—Cecil G. Osborne[34]

Faith in God, no matter how strong, doesn't
entitle us to slack off on prayer and work. In
Ecclesiastes, the farmer was advised to work
both morning and evening, "double planting" so
to speak, to insure a harvest.

West Texas farmers, facing frequent natural
disasters such as boll weevils, drought, and hail-
storms, routinely "double crop" or even diversi-
fy with three or more. If the cotton is damaged,
maybe the sunflowers or grain sorghum will do
well.

Christians should double-crop their lives, too,
working at it early and late for the sake of a good
witness for God. We must keep our fields ex-
posed to the sunshine of God's love by reading
and studying His Word. We must irrigate the
crops by prayer lest they dry up and blow away,

becoming worthless. Then we need to improve the soil by the fertilizer of hard work.

If you sow seed for God wherever and whenever you can and tend it carefully, you will be a fruitful Christian in your church, in your home, and in your community. Your harvest will not fail, and you will be prepared when disaster strikes.

Heavenly Father, may I keep the crops in my life green and growing with the water of prayer and the fertilizer of work. Amen.

---

34. Osborne, p. 88.

46
Perseverance

I press toward the mark for the prize of the high
calling of God in Christ Jesus (Phil. 3:14).

To reach the port of heaven we must sail,
sometimes with the wind, sometimes against it. But
we must sail, and not drift or lie at anchor.
—Oliver Wendell Holmes

A group of teenage boys spent a summer after-
noon in a swift mountain river. They found it
delightful to float with the current. But when the
time came for them to return to camp, swim-
ming upstream was quite a struggle. If they
slowed down to rest, the current pushed them
back. Any progress toward safety required
steady effort, and they found it exhausting.

Do you find life such an effort that you want
to slow down and rest—or maybe quit altogether
and drift? Yet the struggle is necessary. If success
breeds contentment and self-satisfaction, you
become stagnant. If you stop and concentrate on
your failures, you become discouraged and de-
spondent.

The life God wants you to live is one that de-
monstrates that it has been redeemed by Christ.

You should think, act, and talk like a redeemed person—not like the rest of the world. This is true and effective witnessing, showing others what God can do with an ordinary life He has redeemed.

Keep in mind life's tremendous possibilities and go steadily onward. In Christ, God has called you to be His own. You are meant to be a witness for Him and a minister to others. The two calls are not separate; they are the two sides of a single coin. So work faithfully, keeping in view the great reward of the "high calling of God in Christ Jesus."

Lord, sometimes I'm afraid to go on and feel too weak to keep on struggling. Give me faith to stand on tiptoe for Your blessings yet to come. Amen.

47
The Light of Hope

Our Lord Jesus Christ himself, and God, even our Father, which hath loved us, and hath given us everlasting consolation and good hope through grace (2 Thess. 2:16).

Behind the cloud the starlight lurks,
  Through showers the sunbeams fall;
For God, who loved all his works
  Has left this hope for all.
                              —John Greenleaf Whittier

In the mountains of a western state, many men searched for a lost boy. The child was only lightly dressed, and each night the temperature dropped to near freezing. After five days of persistent effort in an extensive, rugged area, little hope remained that the five-year-old would be found alive. Costly expense and many personnel hours had been poured into the search, yet the child's mother pleaded with them to search just one more day.

On the morning of the sixth day, the boy was found. He was awfully tired, cold, hungry, thirsty, and lonely—but alive! Hope was rewarded with joy.

Hope is what's left when strength and reason have departed. Hope is like breathing—it's what we live on. It is light with which we can look into the unnoticed corners of life to find the real assets God has given and the potential He offers for the future. Hope is the ultimate grace of God, God's "everlasting consolation."

To transmit hope in the Lord to others, all of us must keep on breathing the oxygen of God's "good hope." Keep on searching for those on whom others have given up, for abounding is the joy of shining the light on one who can yet be rescued.

Lord Jesus, thank You for the faith, hope, and love with which You send me out. Help me to live triumphantly in the light You give. Amen.

48
"Dust and Ashes"

To give unto them beauty for ashes, the oil of joy for mourning, the garment of praise for the spirit of heaviness (Isa. 61:3).

A very fine singing team of young men with guitars . . . call themselves "Dust & Ashes" and their name relates to their effort to "affirm faith in God and in the worth of persons in the midst of a world where dust and ashes seem to be inescapable realities."
—C. W. Franke[35]

Each spring Americans who live in the Midwest and South, particularly, are threatened by tornados. Impartially these gigantic winds chew to splinters a farmer's isolated barn, a suburb of trailer homes or apartment complexes, or the heart of a city.

Two Texas cities where tornados hit downtown areas have rebuilt with beautiful malls, civic centers, and memorial parks. Those who viewed the destruction can scarcely believe the way those blocks look ten years later. But to rebuild a large area of a city requires vision, cooperation, planning, years of hard work, and vast sums of money.

Christians look around at the moral "dust and ashes" of our society today and are shocked by the ruined lives. Can we "affirm faith in God and in the worth of persons" in the face of moral destruction and imagine how godliness might be restored?

To replace our despair, we need to recover confidence in our Lord and radiance in our lives. This is the aura of our witness—that we walk in calm dependence upon God and reflect the beauty of God's love.

The world today insists upon a demonstration of our faith before it will listen to our words. If we allow the Holy Spirit to make of the ruins in and around our lives a memorial park to Jesus Christ, filled with beauty, joy, and praise, the world will take notice.

Divine Author, inscribe the beauty of Your restoring love on the blank pages of my to-morrows. Amen.

---

35. C. W. Franke, *Defrost Your Frozen Assets,* p. 140.

49
Lighten the Load

Bear ye one another's burdens, and so fulfil the law of Christ (Gal. 6:2).

Because Christ is a part of us, He becomes a part of the friendship and part of that mutual reliance and interdependence. Our neighbor comes to see that we are more than just a neighbor and friend—we are someone who can deal with special problems in a special way because God is our guide.　　　　　　　　—Rosalind Rinker[36]

A government official in India supervised several special schools, including a school for the blind. Concerning that school he commented to a missionary, "Only Christians will do this work." He had experienced the fact that Christians are people who care about other people.

God's love is not merely an "influence." God speaks through the Holy Spirit to our hearts and through us to the hearts of others. We are responsible to share our Christian faith with our fellowmen, thus lightening their burdens. Our continuing response to the living Lord should result in openness and loving concern. If we withhold an appropriate response to God's love, our potential is diminished, and we risk damaging those we love.

It is easy to become so wrapped up in our own

problems that we become selfish and insensitive to the needs of others. We must be aware of our responsibilities and opportunities. We are collaborators with the Great Physician, for He ministers to others through us.

If we remain sensitive to Him and to them, He can pour through the channel of our lives exactly the kind of caring someone else needs to lighten his or her load.

Lord Jesus, make me Your pharmacist so I may dispense Your healing and strengthening love to others. Amen.

---

36. Rosalind Rinker and Harry C. Griffith, *Sharing God's Love,* p. 82.

50
Lighthouse Keepers

You are the world's light—it is impossible to hide a town built on the top of a hill (Matt. 5:14, Phillips).

The Church needs to be four things: a worshiping congregation, a healing communion, a training center, and a missionary sending station.
—Walden Howard[37]

John MacKenzie, a young Scotsman who had offered himself to the Lord for missionary service, sought divine direction about where he should go. "O Lord," he prayed, "send me to the darkest spot on earth!"

That was a deep and valid prayer. After all, for our sakes Jesus Christ went to the darkest spot on earth—Calvary. Nothing could be blacker than that. And as Christ's messengers, we should be willing to represent Him in the darkest places, volunteering for the most difficult assignments He has.

The lighthouse is an appropriate symbol of our shedding God's love in this world. God kindles the fire in each one of us when Jesus comes in, for He is the Light of the world. Then we must tend the flame He gives us.

A lighthouse is designed to guide ships at night, to show them the right lane so they can steer clear of rocks that would wreck them. The light itself need not be large—the beacon is made visible for many miles by the mammoth lens which enlarges and focuses it.

The Holy Spirit is the lens which magnifies our feeble light into a guiding beacon and makes the church a lifesaving agency. We don't have to be specially qualified to witness. After all, our witness is not of ourselves but of Jesus. We don't even have to argue; we have only to let the light Jesus gives be magnified by the Holy Spirit in us.

Strike deep within me, Lord, and remove the inner darkness so Your light may burn brightly in the globe of my body. Amen.

---

37. Howard, p. 116.

51
Sparkling Eyes

Let your light so shine before men, that they may
see your good works, and glorify your Father, which
is in heaven (Matt. 5:16).

Inevitably, I find these "Christians who beam" have
had some kind of deepening experience with God
which has taken them out of the realm of the
ordinary. . . . and are now spontaneously sharing
what they have discovered about what God can
mean and can do in a life.   —Roy Fish[38]

A drama student heard a man speak who had
recently been transformed by the power of
Christ. She commented to another student,
"How is it that the Christians have sparkling
eyes? I'd be a Christian too if I could have eyes
like that."

Eyes have often been called "the windows of
the soul." The inner person is more often revealed by the expression of the eyes than by any
other feature, but sometimes a physical factor
makes a difference.

A grocery store checker had a pretty profile
but sleepy-looking eyes. She seemed withdrawn
and shy. One day a man asked, "What happened
to that girl with the drooping eyelids?"

"I guess I'm the one you mean," the checker

answered. "I had an operation to correct my lazy
eyelids."

Yielding to the operation of divine grace produces both humility and exultation in the Christian. We should be humble because it is Christ's
grace, not our own goodness, that makes us children of God. Our joy over what He has done for
us should light up our eyes so others can see our
redeemed souls shining through to the glory of
God.

Lord, help me beam Your light by yielding
to the Holy Spirit with nothing held back.
Amen.

38. Roy Fish in Worrell, p. 42.

52
When Blessing Falls

O Lord, . . . In this time of our deep need, begin
again to help us, as you did in years gone by
(Hab. 3:2, TLB).

If you want renewal, come out of isolation. Attach
yourself to a group of Christians who have come
alive. . . . Renewal is catching.
    . . . In the spiritual life, there are some things that
can't be worked up. They have to come down.
Renewal is one.   —Bill G. West[39]

The prophet Elijah knew when the end of his
life was approaching as did his companion, Elisha. Elijah repeatedly told Elisha to stay behind,
but the younger man refused: "I swear to God
that I won't leave you." Elijah had performed
many wonders through the power of God, and
Elisha didn't want to miss what might happen
next.

After the two went over the Jordan on dry
ground, Elijah asked, "What wish shall I grant
you before I am taken away?"

"Please grant me twice as much prophetic
power as you have had," Elisha asked boldly.

"You have asked a hard thing," replied Elijah.
"If you see me when I am taken from you, then
you will get your request." (2 Kings 2:4-10, TLB).
Elijah was establishing an inescapable principle:

If you want the blessing, you have to be there when it falls.

Do you want revival—renewal—a fresh touch of the Spirit? Evangelistic work is the permanent duty of the church, but true revival is an outpouring of the Spirit of God upon a group of Christians when and as God chooses. If you absent yourself from Christian fellowship, you may miss some of God's special blessings. You may regret it if you stay away—if you aren't there when it falls.

Holy Spirit, guide me to others in whom You are working that I may join them in prayer for Your special blessings. Amen.

39. Bill G. West, *Free to Be Me*, p. 141.

53
Stumbling Blocks

Take up the stumblingblock out of the way of my people. . . . to revive the spirit of the humble, and to revive the heart of the contrite ones (Isa. 57:14-15).

The renowned Scottish poet Robert Burns once dined at a wayside inn. There a young waiter tripped and spilled a tray of food on a diner. Incensed, the inn keeper fired the waiter on the spot. As the young man, in tears, left the establishment, Burns followed him out the door. Putting his arm around the ex-waiter the poet encouraged him, explaining that it was not the end. This so inspired the young fellow that he redoubled his efforts as a writer. The fired waiter was none other than Walter Scott—later Sir Walter Scott, the famed novelist.

"What happens to you makes a difference to me!" These words reflect the heart of the gospel because we are called to care deeply and unconditionally for others. This is what God does; this is what we are called to do.

The wonder of God's love enriching our lives every moment should flow through all our relationships—at home, at work, on the street, and in the church building. Christian witness consists of doing what is unlikely to occur in anyone's life who is not in touch with the spirit of Christ.

Individuals today hunger deeply to be noticed and to be cared for. We will become stumbling blocks instead of effective witnesses if we lack love. Our witness should not be apologetic or defensive or an awkward duty that calls attention to ourselves rather than to God. The Holy Spirit is available to empower our thoughts, words, and actions with the love of God.

You and I are in the reviving business; carry in your heart the smelling salts of God's love so you can minister to those who are fainting around you. Love is the best medicine for the discouraged, the hurt, the lost, and the hardened.

Father, forgive me the haste and recklessness with which I touch other people's lives. May the sweet aroma of Christ scent each word and deed of mine today. Amen.

54
Tree of Witness

With great power gave the apostles witness of the resurrection of the Lord Jesus: and great grace was upon them all (Acts 4:33).

The church should be more like a filling station where saints are filled up, tuned up, and sent out to witness.   —Gordon R. McLean[40]

A young woman in a soul-winners' class took to heart the challenge to pray for one particular person at least five minutes every day. The following Sunday she brought to class the one for whom she had prayed and who had received Christ—*her husband.*

The first step in witnessing is not talking to people but to God. The apostles' remarkable power to witness was born in prayer. After the ascension of Christ, they waited and prayed ten days before the Holy Spirit descended on them in power. He transformed Christ's followers from cowards to bold witnesses. Thus the message was enhanced by the messengers.

After that upper room experience, those who were there spoke of the risen Christ with supreme confidence and deep conviction. Their witness flowed in widening circles across Jerusalem, through Judea, to the neighboring province of Samaria, and out to the ends of the earth.

Christ's death was for His faltering disciples and for those who heard Peter's first sermon that day in Jerusalem. We rejoice that He died for us, too, but we must remember that He also died for the rest of our generation. We should obey His command to share the good news, but without prayer and pure living we can only hinder the message of God.

Pray—live—tell. These are the flowering stages of the living tree of witness, from its prayer roots to its fragrant blossoms.

> To receive power, to witness with power,
> these are the alternate beats of my heart.
> —E. Stanley Jones

40. McLean, p. 64.

55
"Souls" Are Real People

Beloved, if God so loved us, we ought also to love
one another. . . . If we love one another, God
dwelleth in us, and his love is perfected in us
(1 John 4:11-12).

If these people [who have never experienced a
shred of love] . . . are ever going to have any
serious understanding of God's love and what it
means, they must first experience love in human
terms—in us and through us.   —Findley B. Edge[41]

A book by Crying Wind, a young Navaho
woman, told about some missionaries on her
reservation who did not seem to understand the
Indian people. Although the missionaries
worked hard, they were critical, condescending,
and unloving.

Crying Wind walked five miles to a mission
station where a young missionary couple cared
enough to learn and preach in the Navaho
tongue, to provide clean, mended clothing, and
to give out Bibles in the Navaho language. "They
loved Indians as people," Crying Wind wrote.

People all around us are seeking personal in-
volvement—our lives with their lives. The compassion we show for them reflects the real depth
of our devotion to God. The only motivation that
can support such a demanding ministry is deep

115

awareness that the voice of God calls us to minister in this *place* to this *person* in these *circumstances.*

We must meet people where they are in their helplessness. It is not enough to throw down a rope from the top of a cliff and encourage them to climb up to us. We must descend to them on ropes of love and secure them so God can do the lifting. They must see that we love them just as they are, in human terms, before they can understand what God's love means.

Lord Jesus, give me a thoughtful mind and a willing spirit to reach out friendly hands, with true Christian love, to those in need. Amen.

41. Findley B. Edge, *The Greening of the Church,* p. 140.

56
What We Don't Say

Self-control means controlling the tongue! A quick retort can ruin everything (Prov. 13:3, TLB).

Love is the opening of your life to another. Through sincere interest, simple attention, sensitive listening, compassionate understanding and honest sharing.

An open ear is the only believable sign of an open heart. You learn to understand life—you learn to live—as you learn to listen.

—David Augsburger[42]

Witnessing usually carries the idea of speaking to someone. But there are at least two times when we need to keep our mouths shut: when we are tempted to be angry or make sharp remarks and when we should listen to someone.

It takes caring to "hear" what other people are really saying. Listening is the key to true friendship, and it promotes trust. We all need to talk things out on occasion. Like aspirin, listening seems to help many ailments. Why? Because it gives an assurance of being loved.

Jesus declared that His followers should "love your neighbor as yourself!" (Matt. 19:19, TLB), and that involves listening to others as you would like for them to listen to you.

Perhaps listening may be the most neglected aspect of the evangelical ministry. We talk, talk,

talk about sharing Jesus Christ with others. We often plan carefully the words we are going to speak. Some people even write out their testimonies to use. Yet we too often forget our Christian obligation to participate in the ministry of listening. If we love and listen, others can better understand that God loves them and cares about their problems.

Maybe God gave us a hint when He created us with two ears and one mouth, that one's ears should be open twice as much as one's mouth.

Holy Spirit, infuse me with the joy and poise of Your presence that I may listen with patience and love. Amen.

---

42. David Augsburger, *Seventy Times Seven*, p. 87.

57
Scrubbed Hands

Create in me a clean heart, O God; and renew a
right spirit within me (Ps. 51:10).

Sometimes when you and I read the Word of God,
we may not always understand what we have read!
We may not always remember it, and recall it. But
we shall be clean, for all that. The power the Word
claims is a power to cleanse; and it cleanses the
depths of the personality.   —George Duncan[43]

George Duncan has compared the subconscious with a beautiful garden of memories and also with a garbage bin of accumulated refuse. In this sense, with all the sin of the past dumped there, our subconscious becomes a source of infection of which we are unaware. It needs a cleaning out only God can give.

God desires that we be conformed to the image of the Son, and that means to be characterized by Jesus' holiness and purity. As Christians, we are "called to be saints" (1 Cor. 1:2). This means that we are set apart by God for Himself and that we must endorse it by setting ourselves apart for His service.

If we want to participate in the work God is doing on this earth, we need to be clean, inside and outside. We can't do God's holy work without scrubbed hands. If our motives and desires are not pure, neither will our actions be pure. Until one has a pure heart, one can't live a pure life.

How can we secure this needed cleansing? The principle is given in Psalm 119:11: "Thy word have I hid in mine heart, that I might not sin against thee." In the New Testament, the Word of God is frequently compared with water which is applied to our inner beings by the Holy Spirit to cleanse the depths of our personalities. Each time we say yes to the indwelling Spirit, we open ourselves to the Spirit's cleansing and draw on His power.

Holy Spirit, cleanse me and make me pure like Jesus—then give me power to reflect Him to others. Amen.

---

43. Duncan, p. 106.

58
Arms of Fellowship

If you believe that Jesus is the Christ—that he is
God's Son and your Savior—then you are a child of
God. And all who love the Father love his children
too (1 John 5:1, TLB).

It is important to wrap loving arms of fellowship
around the baby Christian. After all, he'll probably
lose all his old friends within the first three months
he is a Christian. If you don't include him in your
social gatherings, where will he go for activity and
sharing?
—Ralph Neighbour[44]

Jesus asked the disciples, "If ye love them
which love you, what reward have ye?" (Matt.
5:46). The implication reaches to those who need
food and clothing and to those who are lonely
and need an atmosphere of thoughtfulness and
love.

New Christians have been compared to babies, and "follow-up" has been called "spiritual
pediatrics." Babies require much special care,
and we can't throw spiritual babies into a church
and expect them to look out for themselves. The
Sunday School lesson and the pastor's sermon
need to be "strong meat" sometimes, and the
new Christian must have "baby food" like John
3:16 and how to find the books of the Bible.

The new Christian who does not have a Christian background, particularly, must be made to

feel a part of the family. A few words of welcome from the pastor over the microphone aren't enough. Each member is responsible to be friendly, to act in love toward the new Christian, perhaps to assume special responsibility for him or her. Notice what often happens at a church fellowship: those who have known each other for years stand talking to one another, but around the fringes sit the quiet people, the elderly, and the newcomers. Do they really have "fellowship"?

Do we seek out the people whose friendship we want or the people who need our friendship? Do we love all God's children?

Lord, give me the courage to look up some chair sitters and love them for You. Amen.

---

44. Ralph W. Neighbour, Jr., *Journey into Discipleship* (Atlanta: Home Mission Board of the Southern Baptist Convention, 1976), p. 88.

59
"Reach Out and Touch"

Beloved, let us love one another, for love is of God;
and every one that loveth is born of God, and
knoweth God. He that loveth not knoweth not God;
for God is love (1 John 4:7-8).

You are the king of your own personal kingdom; and
it is the will of the Father, after you have set your
own kingdom in order, that you reach out and
embrace all whom you can. It can be a word, a
gesture, a touch, encouragement, love.
—Cecil G. Osborne[45]

More than ever loneliness is characteristic of Americans. When we walk down city streets or through a shopping mall, we notice innumerable lonely faces. One of the major reasons is that many people have been uprooted and detached from their family relationships. Even in our affluent society, too many individuals feel isolated and unloved. Listen to popular music with its plaintive, lonely voices. Look at the crowds on television—do they have happy faces?

God meant for us to help one another, to love one another with godlike love. The only way He can show His love to those who don't know Him is through us. If our Christian experience matters to us, we must tell everyone we can about our Lord.

Are you reaching out to anyone? First of all,

reach out to your fellow Christians who need your love. Who of your friends are weary and despairing and need encouragement? Have you cared enough to find out? Others who need God's light and love through you may be those unpleasant neighbors, people at work with broken homes or ruined lives, strangers with hungry souls. Are you sensitive to their suffering? Do you respond by loving them and inviting them to share their problems with you?

Lord, help me to shine God's light into the darkness around me and demonstrate Your love to those who are loveless. Amen.

---

45. Osborne, p. 37.

60
The Innkeepers

A certain Samaritan, . . . had compassion on him,
And . . . bound up his wounds, . . . and set him on
his own beast, and brought him to an inn, and took
care of him (Luke 10:33-34).

Things were meant to be used; people were meant
to be loved. Much of our trouble comes when we
reverse the two.   —Gordon R. McLean[46]

D. T. Niles, an eloquent preacher from Sri
Lanka, suggests that the true imagery of the
good Samaritan story might be a bit different
from how we usually hear it. "He pointed out
that Christians are not the Samaritans searching
for battered humanity to bring them to whole-
ness," says Lewis Abbot. "Rather, Christians are
to be the innkeepers. Jesus is the Samaritan. He
finds the battered person. He trusts us with him.
We become innkeepers as laborers together
with God."[47]

Our ministry can be compared to that of innkeepers in several ways. We are to be hospitable
and welcoming. We feed new Christians with
the Bread of life, the Word of God. We comfort
them with the rest and security He has given us.
We act as guides to those who are struggling to

find their way around in a strange new place—and provide for them a "home away from home."

To love people results in wanting to help them in time of need. Jesus loves people, and He sends them to us to help Him show that love concretely—to be Jesus' hands and feet, His mouth and ears. In this sense, all Christians might be called innkeepers and ministers.

Christ continues to transform our lives on an individual basis, usually through the ministry of other people, until we are full grown and equipped to serve as ministers to those around us. No matter what specific vocation we pursue, because Christ is our Lord we are all ministers to one another and especially to those who are still outside Him.

Holy Spirit, lead me in the path of my Lord where I will glorify God and fulfill His destiny for me. Amen.

---

46. McLean, p. 80.
47. Lewis Abbot in Worrell, p. 30.

Bibliography

Angell, James W. *Yes Is a World.* Waco: Word Books, 1974.

Augsburger, David. *Seventy Times Seven: The Freedom of Forgiveness.* Chicago: Moody Press, 1970.

Baughman, Ray E. *The Abundant Life.* Chicago: Moody Press, 1959.

Beckwith, Paul, editor. *Hymns.* Chicago: Inter-Varsity Christian Fellowship Press, 1950.

Duncan, George. *Mastery in the Storm.* Fort Washington, Pa.: Christian Literature Crusade, 1965.

Edge, Findley B. *The Greening of the Church.* Waco, Tex.: Word Books, 1971.

Franke, C. W. *Defrost Your Frozen Assets.* Waco, Tex.: Word Books, 1969.

Franzmann, Martin H. *Alive with the Spirit.* Saint Louis, Mo.: Concordia Publishing House, 1973.

Graham, Billy. *Day-by-Day with Billy Graham.* Edited by J. W. Brown. Minneapolis, Minn.: World Wide Publications, 1976.

Howard, Walden. *Nine Roads to Renewal.* Waco, Tex.: Word Books, 1967.

Hudson, R. Lofton. *Grace Is Not a Blue-Eyed Blonde.* Waco, Tex.: Word Books, 1968.

_____. *Helping Each Other Be Human.* Waco, Tex.: Word Books, 1970.

Jones, E. Stanley. *The Art of Mastering Life.* Nashville, Tenn.: Abingdon Press, 1953.

_____. *Growing Spiritually.* Nashville, Tenn.: Abingdon Press, 1953.

Larson, Bruce. *Thirty Days to a New You.* Grand Rapids, Mich.: Zondervan Publishing House, 1974.

Lockerbie, Jeanette. *Fifty Plus.* Old Tappan, N.J.: Fleming H. Revell Company, 1976.

MacGorman, Jack W. *The Gifts of the Spirit.* Nashville, Tenn.: Broadman Press, 1974.

McLean, Gordon R. *Where the Love Is.* Waco, Tex.: Word Books, 1973.

Neighbour, Ralph W., Jr. *Journey into Discipleship.* Atlanta: Home Mission Board of the Southern Baptist Convention, 1976.

_____. *The Touch of the Spirit.* Nashville, Tenn.: Broadman Press, 1972.

Osborne, Cecil G. *You're in Charge.* Waco, Tex.: Word Books, 1973.

Raines, Robert A. *Soundings.* New York: Harper & Row, 1970.

Ramm, Bernard L. *Rapping About the Spirit.* Waco, Tex.: Word Books, 1974.

Redpath, Alan. *Victorious Christian Service.* Westwood, N.J.: Fleming H. Revell Company, 1957.

Rinker, Rosalind and Griffith, Harry C. *Sharing God's Love.* Grand Rapids, Mich.: Zondervan Publishing House, 1976.

Tournier, Paul. *The Adventure of Living.* New York: Harper & Row, 1965.

_____. *Escape from Loneliness.* New York: Harper & Row, 1967.

West, Bill G. *Free to Be Me.* Waco, Tex.: Word Books, 1971.

Whiston, Lionel A. *Enjoy the Journey.* Waco, Tex.: Word Books, 1972.

Worrell, George E., editor. *Resources for Renewal.* Nashville, Tenn.: Broadman Press, 1975.